The Art of
Cooking
With
Quinoa

Maria Baez Kijac

Eighth Printing 2009

ISBN 0-9633303-0-6

Published by PM Publishing
6 Warwick Lane
Lincolnshire, IL 60069
Printed in the United States of America

Table of Contents

Foreword...V

Sources for Quinoa..VII

Nutritional Profile of Quinoa....................................VIII

Instructions for Washing and Cooking Quinoa.............X

Basic Boiled Quinoa..XI

Hors d'Oeuvres...1
    Tamarillo, Lupini Beans and Quinoa Salsa.................2
    Pancakes, Chinese Style 3
    Snow Peas Stuffed with Shrimp and Quinoa 4

Soups 5
    Quinoa Chowder...6
    Tomato and Onion Soup with Quinoa 7
    Vegetable Soup, Peruvian Style............................8
    Cream of Broccoli Soup with Quinoa 10
    Cream of Quinoa Soup.......................................11

Main Courses and Side Dishes.......................................13
    Crustless Asparagus-Quinoa Quiche 14
    Quinoa Souffle..15
    Quinoa-Pasta with Vegetable Sauce......................16
    Quinoa-Pasta Gratineed....................................17
    Quinoa with Chicken, Spanish Style......................18
    Quinoa Pilaff...19
    Savoy Cabbage Patties 20
    Quinoa, Chicken and Black Bean Salad 21
    Wild Rice with Shrimp and Quinoa Salad...............22
    Korean Style Salad..23
    Creamy Quinoa...24
    Dinner Rolls 25

Desserts & Drinks..27
    Quinoa Pudding with Currants 28
    Pineapple-Quinoa Dessert..................................29
    Quinoa Fruit Bars 30
    Brown Sugar Nut Balls.....................................31
    Quinoa and Cornstarch Dainties 32
    Atole with Almonds and Quinoa.........................33
    Fruit-Quinoa Drink...34

Foreword

From the Incas who first cultivated the "Mother Grain" five centuries ago, to its modern proponents who consider it a "supergrain" and a "wonder grain", quinoa (pronounced 'Kee-no-a') is a cereal of superlatives. The Incas revered the grain for its nutritional value and the strength-producing energy to sustain hard labor at high altitudes. According to a legend, quinoa was the remains of a heavenly banquet, and each planting season began with the Inca rulers planting the first row with a golden spade.

The decline of quinoa began half a millenium ago with the fall of the Incas. Their Spanish conquerors rejected the grain as "Indian food" and suppressed its use to the point where it nearly disappeared. Recently, however, quinoa emerged from relative obscurity in its native Andean highlands, thanks to the growth of health-and-nutrition consciousness of recent decades. Its rediscovery can be credited to scientific research and continuing effort to find suitable foods to fight the world's famines. Indigenous to the Western slopes of the Andes of Ecuador, Peru and Bolivia, quinoa is now imported to this country, as well as cultivated in Colorado, New Mexico, northern California, Washington and Oregon.

There are about 1800 varieties of quinoa, which range in size from as small as a grain of sand to the size of sesame seed, and in color from ivory to yellow, brown and black. The plant grows at high altitudes and is frost resistant thanks to the size of its germ, or embryo, which is enormous when compared to that of other grains. The latter also explains its amazing nutrient profile, characterized by an outstanding balance of protein, minerals, and vital amino acids. Interest in quinoa is not merely a short-lived fashion of health food faddists. Some advocates even claim medicinal, stamina-giving and "spiritual" qualities. Rather, its centuries-old history as a staple protein for hardy mountain tribes, and modern laboratory evaluation of its nutritional content fully establish the grain's health credentials and bring it very close to an ideal "whole" food.

From a cook's point of view, quinoa is an extremely versatile grain, suitable for almost any kind of dish. It is a good substitute for rice and bulghur and can be used in salads, soups, stews, croquettes, casseroles, or to stuff vegetables and make desserts. When stored in a cool dry place, quinoa's one-year shelf life also makes it handy to keep in bulk. It is important to remember, however, that the grains need to be thoroughly rinsed in order to remove the naturally-occurring substance called saponin. Saponin is a sticky, soaplike material, bitter to the taste, that coats the grains. Produced by the plant itself, it serves to discourage insects, birds, and other predators. Although most quinoa is brought to the market with the saponin largely removed, a final thorough rinse is necessary in the kitchen. Many first time users of the grain are unnecessarily discouraged by a bitter tasting quinoa dish, due merely to inadequate rinsing.

Since quinoa does not contain the gluten of grains such as wheat, it is a valuable alternative for those who suffer from grain allergies. Its quantity of high-quality protein makes quinoa a desirable alternative for vegetarians and others who seek to limit their intake of meats or other animal protein. Be careful, however, not to overindulge, as it could cause stomach discomfort for some people. When apprised of these qualities, health food enthusiasts and food professionals, including hospital dieticians, all wished to learn more.

The recipe selection represents a wide range of countries of origin. Each recipe has been thoroughly tested at least four times. Nutritional values given for each recipe are approximate and are for general guidelines only. When an ingredient is listed as 'optional', or 'to taste', it is not counted in the nutritional break-down. Margarine was used instead of butter. Recipes were tested at sea level.

Sources for Quinoa

Eden Foods, Inc.
701 Tecumseh Road
Clinton, Michigan 49236

Telephone: 517/456-7424
Fax: 517/456-7025

Arrowhead Mills
Box 2059
Hereford, Texas 79045-2059

Telephone: 806/364-0730
Fax: 806/364-8242

Quinoa Corporation
P.O. Box 1039
Torrance, CA 90505

Quinoa Corporation
2300 Central Ave., Suite G
Boulder, CO 80301

Telephone: 800/237-2304

Dean & Deluca
110 Green Street, Suite 304
New York, NY 10012

Telephone: 800/221-7714

Natural Food Stores.

Some specialty supermarkets, such as Treasure Island and Sunset Foods in the Chicago area.

Nutritional Profile of Quinoa

This highly nutritious grain contains almost twice the amount of protein as compared to other grains. Unlike other grains, it contains all the amino acids that are absent from most plant proteins. Quinoa is as rich in calcium as milk, but without cholesterol, has much less starch than rice or wheat, and a half-cup of cooked grain has less than 100 calories.

Determining exact nutritional properties of quinoa is not possible on a universal basis because of the variations between individual strains, soil conditions, method employed in removing saponin, and many other factors. In general, South American quinoa has higher nutritional values than its North American counterparts at this time.

As a general guide we are giving the following table from Eden Foods, Inc., a distributor of a Quinoa variety from Ecuador. Two ounces of dry Quinoa (approximately 1 cup cooked) will yield the following:

Nutrition Information

Serving Size	2	oz.	Fat	4	g
Servings per package	7		Cholesterol	0 mg/100	g
Calories	200		Sodium	Less than 30	mg
Protein	8	g	Potassium	270	mg
Carbohydrate	38	g			

Percentage of U.S. RDA

Protein	10	%	Iron	15	%
Vitamin A	*		Vitamin D	*	
Vitamin C	*		Vitamin E	6	%
Thiamine (Vitamin B-1)	25	%	Vitamin B-6	15	%
Riboflavin (B-2)	10	%	Vitamin B-12	*	
Niacin	2	%	Phosphorus	25	%
Calcium	2	%	Zinc	8	%

* Contains less than 2% of the U.S. RDA of these nutrients.

Total Amino Acid Profile
(milligrams per gram)

Aspartic Acid	12.50	Glutamatic Acid	20.60
Leucine	9.03	Lysine	8.43
Tyrosine	3.82	Proline	6.19
Isoleucine	5.13	Tryptophan	1.69
Threonine	5.24	Glycine	8.27
Phenylalanine	5.74	Arginine	11.10
Serine	6.37	Alanine	6.21
Histidine	4.96	Methionine	1.68
Cycstine	1.39	Valine	6.29

According to another organization (INIAP of Ecuador, South America), quinoa also contains, in grams per 100 grams:

Ash	2.90
Fiber	3.90

Another item worth mentioning is that most of the many different proteins are synthesized within the human body from amino acids. There are eight essential amino acids that must come from external food sources, but all eight must come together and in a proper quantity ratio between each other to produce desirable quality of protein. Unlike most of the foods, quinoa matches these requirements almost to perfection.

Instructions for Washing and Cooking Quinoa

Because not all the saponin is removed from the quinoa when packaged for distribution, **thorough washing of the quinoa before cooking is recommended.** Since brands vary depending on their processing techniques, it is hard to tell how much washing or rinsing a particular variety may need. The best rule to follow it to **keep rinsing until water comes out clear.**

Put quinoa in a fine mesh strainer that fits on top of a bowl. Pick and discard any impurities. Place strainer in bowl, fill with cold water. With your fingers rub quinoa grains until water becomes sudsy and cloudy. Sudsy water denotes the presence of saponin. Lift strainer, discard water from bowl. Repeat process until water comes out clear, it takes about 3 rinsings.

In Ecuador people use a method that is quite effective for quinoa with a heavy saponin content. Pick and discard any impurities from quinoa, sift to remove as much sand as possible. Put in blender, add 2 cups water and turn machine on-off a couple of times. Water will be sudsy and cloudy. Drain through a fine mesh sieve, repeat the operation as many times as needed until water comes out clear.

Now quinoa is ready for cooking. When the recipe calls for cooked quinoa for salads, cook the quinoa for 12 minutes, or until grains are transparent throughout, in at least double the amount of boiling water that is needed for **Basic Boiled Quinoa,** and then drain. The quinoa grains cooked in this fashion seem to be less sticky. When adding quinoa to soups that have some acidic ingredients, allow more than 15 minutes to cook.

I prefer to cook quinoa without any salt so it can be used for making sweet or savory dishes. Many people also believe salt prevents quinoa from increasing in volume.

The salt used throughout the recipes is coarse salt (kosher) because it does not contain additives, and its flavor is better and more intense. The amounts given in the recipes can be varied according to the dietary needs.

BASIC BOILED QUINOA   **Makes about 4 cups**

2 cups water*
1 cup quinoa, thoroughly rinsed

Bring water to the boil in a 2-quart heavy saucepan. Add quinoa, bring back to a boil, cover, cook over medium heat for 12 minutes or until quinoa has absorbed all the water. Remove from the heat, fluff, cover and let it stand for 5 minutes. Should the quinoa taste bitter after cooking, rinse with cold water until the bitterness disappears. Drain thoroughly, return to saucepan, cover and steam until dry, about 5 minutes.

When the recipe calls for cooked quinoa, use this method of cooking. It yields about 4 cups cooked quinoa. If not using right away, store in a covered container in the refrigerator, it keeps fresh for 3 to 4 days. Excellent as a breakfast cereal, just microwave individual portions and serve with milk and raw sugar. Always keep some cooked quinoa in the refrigerator, it comes handy to make fruit drinks, omelettes, etc.

Quinoa can also be toasted to obtain a more intense flavor. Toast for a few minutes in a little butter or oil, stirring constantly, before proceding with the recipe.

* For a firmer grain use $1^3/_4$ cups water.

Per Cup: 150 Calories, 3 g. Fat, 0.38 mg. Cholesterol, 12.5 mg. Sodium, 1.7 g. Fiber, 6 g. Protein.

My Preferred Method

I discovered this by sheer accident, and it remains my favorite method of cooking quinoa: Bring quinoa and water to the boil, cook for a couple of minutes, remove from the heat and let stand, covered for 30 minutes. At this point the quinoa will be fully cooked – if there is some water left drain it, return quinoa to the saucepan, cover it and steam until dry, about 5 minutes.

NOTE: It is important for this method to use the cooking pan that conducts heat well, such as cast iron, heavy aluminum, etc., fitted with a tight lid.

Hors D'Oeuvres

TAMARILLO, LUPINI BEAN
AND QUINOA SALSA
Makes 2 cups

This very unusual and delicious salsa comes from Ecuador and combines the taste and texture of grain, fruit and legume unique to Ecuador. Pureed tamarillo fruit and quinoa form the base for this salsa, which in many variations is a standard at the Ecuadorean table. Chopped lupini beans add a nutty counterpoint. Serve as a dip with blue corn chips or on grilled fish or chicken—terrific either way!

2	Tamarillos, firm, or
2	large Pear shaped Tomatoes (about 6 ozs.)
1	cup Water
1/2	cup cooked Quinoa
1	teaspoon Olive Oil
1	teaspoon fresh Lemon Juice
1/4	teaspoon Coarse Salt
1/4	teaspoon Sugar
1/2	cup bottled Lupini Beans, peeled and chopped
1/2	cup finely chopped Red Onion
1-2	tablespoons finely chopped fresh Cilantro (Coriander)
	Freshly grated Black Pepper
	Hot Sauce such as El Habanero
	Blue Corn Chips

Blanch tamarillos or tomatoes in boiling water for a few seconds, rinse with cold water and peel. Split in half crosswise, remove seeds with teaspoon, rinse shells well, cut up in small pieces and cook with quinoa and water for 5 minutes after it comes to the boil. Cool and puree in blender until smooth.

Transfer to a non-reactive bowl, mix with oil, lemon juice, salt, sugar, lupini beans, onion and cilantro, season with black pepper and hot sauce to taste and chill until needed. If salsa is too thick, thin it with a little water. Serve with blue corn chips. This salsa is also wonderful on grilled fish or chicken.

NOTES: Tamarillos, a tart red or yellow fruit, are about the size and shape of an egg, pointed on the end opposite to the stem. It is a seasonal fruit that appears in the markets in May and are available for 3 months. Blanched and seeded they freeze very well.

Lupini Beans are extremely high in protein and are available in the Italian section of supermarkets. Sodium content of these beans was not available, therefore it is not reflected in the sodium count.

Per Tablespoon: 12 Calories, 0.3 g. Fat, 0 mg. Cholesterol, 0.8 mg. Sodium, 0.8 g. Protein, 0.3 g. Fiber.

QUINOA PANCAKES, CHINESE STYLE   Makes 12

These were inspired by the delicious pancakes my friend Kurt Youngman served as appetizers in his restaurant the Meandering Mandarin, except that the basic ingredient is quinoa, rather than flour. Delicious when served plain, they are even better with a dollop of sour cream and caviar on top.

- 1 cup Cooked Quinoa
- 1 teaspoon Sesame Oil
- 2 tablespoons Flour
- 1/4 cup finely chopped Scallions (use some of the green)
- 1/4 cup finely chopped Water Chestnuts
- 2 ounces fresh Shrimp, finely chopped
- 1 Egg, lightly beaten
- 1 teaspoon light Soy Sauce (low sodium)
  Few drops Hot Sauce

- 1 tablespoon Vegetable Oil for cooking pancakes

In a mixing bowl toss quinoa with sesame oil. Combine with the rest of ingredients.

Heat a pancake griddle, preferably non-stick, over medium heat. coat with 1 teaspoon of oil and drop heaping tablespoons of quinoa mixture over hot griddle, spreading with a spatula to make a 2-1/2 to 3-inch circle. Cook for a few seconds on both sides until golden brown. Serve right away plain or with a dollop of sour cream. For a festive occasion top the sour cream with a sprinkling of black or red caviar.

Per Pancake: 44.5 Calories, 1.5 g. Fat, 32 mg. Cholesterol, 31 mg. Sodium, 2.2 g. Protein, 0.2 g. Fiber.

SNOW PEAS STUFFED WITH
SHRIMP AND QUINOA
Makes 36

A superb way to introduce quinoa to your friends. This colorful platter is more than an hors d'oeuvre, it is a conversation piece. The stuffing also can be used with cherry tomatoes as a variation.

2	ounces cooked Shrimp, finely chopped
3/4	cup cooked Quinoa
2	tablespoons minced Scallions (some green included)
1	tablespoon minced fresh Cilantro
3	tablespoons Mayonnaise
2	teaspoons Ketchup
1	teaspoon fresh Lemon Juice
1/4	teaspoon Worchestershire Sauce
1/2	teaspoon Dijon Mustard
1/8	teaspoon White Pepper
	Cayenne Pepper
	Coarse Salt
40	Snow Peas (Pea Pods), or Cherry Tomatoes

Thoroughly mix shrimp with rest of ingredients through white pepper. Season with cayenne and salt to taste. If mixture is runny add a bit more of quinoa or bread crumbs. Chill.

Choose only the best snow peas. String and blanch them in boiling water until the color turns bright green, about 30 seconds. Drain, rinse with cold water, dry with paper towels. With a small, thin knife split open the side opposite the side with the tiny peas.

Stuff the snow peas with the shrimp mixture using a small spoon. Carefully wipe off any excess on the outside and place them on a tray lined with paper towels, cover and refrigerate until needed. To serve arrange them in a spoke fashion on a serving platter lined with a paper doilie. A tomato flower in the center enhances the presentation.

Filling per Hors d'oeuvre: 10.7 Calories, 1.0 g. Fat, 3.7 mg. Cholesterol, 12.0 mg. Sodium, 0.5 g. Protein, 0.04 g. Fiber.

Soups

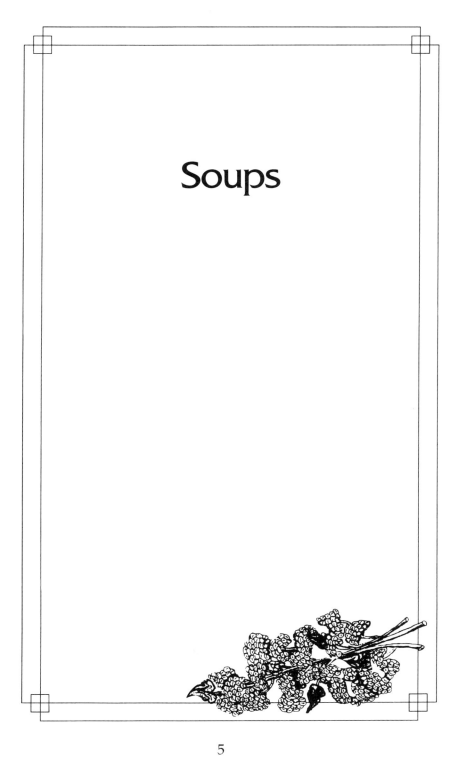

QUINOA CHOWDER   **Makes 8 cups**

The people of Latin America, especially Ecuador and Peru, are extremely fond of potato chowders. Prized for their simplicity and wholesomeness, they are often referred to as "comfort food". This nutritious and filling quinoa chowder is served hot and it will satisfy the heartiest appetite when served as a main course.

>   2 tablespoons unsalted Butter or Margarine
>   1 cup chopped Onions
>   2 cloves Garlic, minced
>   1/2 teaspoon Paprika
>   4 cups Hot Water (or chicken or vegetable bouillon)
>   1 lb. boiling Potatoes, cut up in 1-inch pieces
>   1 cup fresh or frozen Corn Kernels
>   1 cup Low Fat 2% Milk
>   2 cups cooked Quinoa
>   1/4 lb. (1 cup packed) grated Cheddar Cheese
>   1 teaspoon Coarse Salt
>   1/4 teaspoon White Pepper
>   2 Eggs, lightly beaten
>
>   Minced fresh Parsley or Cilantro Leaves (Coriander)
>   1 Avocado, diced (optional)

In a 4-quart saucepan melt butter or margarine over medium heat, add onion and sauté for 10 minutes stirring occasionally. Add garlic and paprika, sauté for a couple of minutes. Add water or bouillon, potatoes and corn, and simmer for 15 minutes or until potatoes are tender. Add milk and quinoa, heat up until it comes to the boil, add eggs, cheese, salt and pepper, stir until cheese is melted and eggs have set. Serve hot, garnished with parsley or coriander, and a few pieces of optional avocado. This soup can be used as a first course or as a main course.

Per Cup: 214 Calories, 9.2 g. Fat, 85.8 mg. Cholesterol, 362.7 mg. Sodium, 9.2 g. Protein, 0.6 g. Fiber

TOMATO AND ONION SOUP WITH QUINOA

Serves 8

This is a delicious soup I adapted from a Cordon Bleu recipe. In the summertime, when the tomatoes are at its peak, my friends make big batches of it and freeze in different size containers to enjoy on the cold winter nights.

- 1 lb. Tomatoes, peeled, seeded and chopped
- 2 tablespoons Tomato Paste
- 1 Bay Leaf
- 1 Garlic Clove

- 2 cups thinly sliced Onions
- 2 tablespoons Olive Oil

- 4 cups Water
- 4 Chicken or Vegetable Bouillon cubes
- 1/3 cup Quinoa, thoroughly rinsed
- 1/2 teaspoon Sugar
- 1/4 teaspoon freshly ground Black Pepper
  Coarse Salt (optional)

- 1 Tomato peeled, seeded and julienned

Put the tomatoes, tomato paste, bay leaf and garlic in a 2-quart saucepan, cover and simmer for 15 minutes. Remove bay leaf and puree the mixture in a blender or food processor. Strain and reserve.

Put onions and oil in a 4-quart saucepan, cover and cook over low heat, stirring occasionally for 30 minutes, without letting them brown. Add the tomato puree, water, bouillon cubes, quinoa, sugar, pepper and salt to taste. Bring to the boil, cover and simmer for 30 minutes. If too thick, add more water and simmer for a few minutes. Add tomato, bring back to the boil and serve.

Per Serving: 109 Calories,   4.9 g. Fat,   0.6 mg. Cholesterol,   398 mg. Sodium, 4.6 g. Protein,   1.3 g. Fiber

---

VEGETABLE SOUP, PERUVIAN STYLE   Serves 10

Peruvians make wonderful, tasty soups that are usually spiced up with hot chili peppers, which may be omitted. Cilantro and mint lend an exotic undertone that gives the soup its special Peruvian character and taste. This nourishing soup is a complete meal in itself and all it needs is some crusty bread to go along with it.

3/4	lb. Beef Brisket*
10	cups Water
2	tablespoons Vegetable Oil
2	medium Onions, finely chopped
2	cloves Garlic, minced
2	medium Tomatoes, peeled, seeded and chopped
1-2	Hot Chili Peppers, seeded and chopped
1	teaspoon Paprika
1/2	teaspoon ground Cumin
1	teaspoon Dry Oregano Leaves
1	teaspoon Coarse Salt
1/2	teaspoon Sugar
1/2	teaspoon freshly ground Black Pepper
1	large Carrot, diced 1/4-inch
4	cups coarsely chopped Cabbage
2	medium Potatoes, peeled and diced 1-inch
1/2	cup Quinoa, thoroughly rinsed
2	cups Winter Squash, peeled and diced 1-inch
1	cup fresh or frozen Corn Kernels
1	cup fresh or frozen Peas

Fresh Cilantro and Mint, minced

In a large soup kettle put water and brisket, bring to a boil. Skim off the froth as it raises to the top, reduce the heat to low, cover and simmer for 1 hour or until meat is tender. Remove meat, cut into 1/2" pieces, return to the pot.

In a skillet heat oil over medium heat, add onions, garlic, tomatoes, and chili peppers and sauté for 10 minutes. Stir in paprika, cumin, oregano, salt, sugar, and pepper, sauté for a couple of minutes. Add to soup, together with carrots, cabbage, potatoes and quinoa. Cook for 15 minutes, then add squash, corn, and peas, cook covered for 15 minutes or until vegetables are tender. Correct seasoning with salt and pepper to taste. Add boiling water if too thick, simmer for a few minutes to blend flavors. Serve hot, garnished with cilantro and mint. This soup improves if made the day before.

*Note: Omit brisket for a vegetarian soup. Instead add 2 tablespoons of vegetable bouillon concentrate, if desired, and omit salt.

If using frozen corn and peas, add them 5 minutes before the end of cooking time.

Per Serving: 227 Calories, 10.0 g. Fat, 38.0 mg. Cholesterol, 261.2 mg. Sodium, 16.7 g. Protein, 2.3 g. Fiber

CREAM OF BROCCOLI SOUP
WITH QUINOA

Makes 12 cups

A soup for all seasons, this variation on a classic cream of broccoli is equally at home when served hot for an elegant dinner party, or chilled for a picnic.

2 tablespoons Unsalted Butter or Margarine
1 cup chopped Onions
1 cup thinly sliced Leek (use 2-inches of the green)
2 Garlic cloves, minced

1-1/2 pounds Broccoli
3 cups Hot Water
4 Chicken or Vegetable Bouillon cubes

1 cup Low Fat 2% Milk
1/2 cup Whipping Cream (optional)
1/4 teaspoon White Pepper
1/2 teaspoon Dry Mustard
1 teaspoon Lemon Juice
2 cups cooked Quinoa
Coarse Salt

Cayenne Pepper

In a heavy saucepan melt butter or margarine over moderate heat, add onions, leek and garlic, cover and cook without browning, stirring occasionally for 10 minutes.

Rinse and trim broccoli, separating the flowerets from the stalks. Slice the stalks into 1/2-inch rounds.

To the saucepan with the onions add water, bouillon cubes and broccoli stalks, bring to the boil and simmer for 15 minutes. Add flowerets, simmer for 10 more minutes after it comes back to the boil. Pureé the soup in a blender or food processor, pass it through a sieve, return to saucepan, add milk, optional cream, pepper, mustard, lemon juice and quinoa. Bring the soup back to a simmer, add more milk or water if too thick. Season with salt to taste. Serve hot with a sprinkling of cayenne, or chilled cold.

Per Cup: 81.3 Calories, 3.2 g. Fat, 1.8 mg. Cholesterol, 410.6 mg. Sodium, 3.6 g. Protein, 1.1 g. Fiber.

CREAM OF QUINOA SOUP   Serves 8

*The unusual use of peanut butter in this creamy soup adds a seasoning
note that, along with cumin, makes it very special. A popular soup in
Ecuador, it is both rich and satisfying.*

> 1 cup Quinoa, thoroughly rinsed
> 4 cups Hot Water (or chicken or vegetable bouillon)
>
> 1 tablespoon Unsalted Butter or Margarine
> 1 tablespoon Vegetable Oil
> 1 cup thinly sliced Leek (white part only)
> 1/2 cup sliced Onions
> 1 teaspoon Paprika
> 1/2 teaspoon Coarse Salt
> 1/4 teaspoon White Pepper
> 1/4 teaspoon ground Cumin
> 2 tablespoons smooth Peanut Butter
>
> 2 cups Low-Fat 2% Milk
> 1/2 cup Whipping Cream (optional)
>
> 1/4 cup Grated Parmesan Cheese

Cook quinoa according to the **Basic Boiled Quinoa** recipe.
Remove from the heat and set aside.

In a 9-inch skillet heat butter or margarine and oil. Add leek and
onion, cover and cook vegetables over low heat, stirring
occasionally, without letting them color, for about 20 minutes.
Season with paprika, salt, pepper and cumin. Transfer to a blender
or food processor, add peanut butter and quinoa, process until
smooth. Return mixture to saucepan and add milk and optional
cream. Bring to a simmer over low heat, stirring occasionally. If
soup is too thick thin it with a little milk or stock. Serve hot in soup
bowls garnished with a dust of Parmesan cheese.

This soup can also be served without pureeing.

Per Serving: 178 Calories, 6.5 g. Fat, 6.7 mg. Cholesterol, 204.6 mg. Sodium,
7.5 g. Protein, 1.1 g. Fiber

Main Courses
And
Side Dishes

CRUSTLESS ASPARAGUS-QUINOA QUICHE

Serves 10

Cooked quinoa with lightly beaten eggs lends a soufflelike texture to this remarkable quiche. Pungent with parmesan and Swiss cheese, the quiche melts in your mouth. Excellent as a party appetizer or luncheon dish, make plenty beforehand because it's easy to make a meal of it.

- 12 Asparagus Spears
- 2 tablespoons Butter or Margarine
- 1/4 cup thinly sliced Scallions (use some of the green)
- 2 tablespoons chopped Pimento
- 1/2 teaspoons dry Basil Leaves
- pinch of Nutmeg
- 1/4 teaspoon White Pepper

- 2 cups cooked Quinoa
- 1/4 lb. shredded Swiss Cheese (1 cup packed)
- 1/4 cup grated Parmesan Cheese
- 4 Eggs, lightly beaten
- 1 cup Milk
- 1/2 cup Whipping Cream
- Coarse Salt

Remove tough ends from asparagus. Cut 10 asparagus 3-inches down from the tips and parboil 3 minutes. Cut remaining asparagus in 1/2-inch pieces. Melt butter or margarine in a skillet, add chopped asparagus and sauté for 5 minutes. Add scallions, pimento, basil, nutmeg and pepper, sauté stirring for a couple of minutes.

In a large bowl mix sauteed asparagus with rest of ingredients, seasoning with salt to taste. Transfer mixture to a well buttered 10-inch quiche pan that has been placed on a round pizza baking sheet and bake in a preheated 400° oven for 25 minutes. Remove from oven and arrange asparagus tips on top in spoke fashion, pressing down a little. Bake 15 more minutes or until quiche browns and puffs. Let quiche cool for a few minutes before cutting into 10 wedges. Quiche can be prepared 1 or 2 days ahead and reheated in a 350° oven for 20 minutes.

Per Serving: 173 Calories, 9.7 g. Fat, 133.5 mg. Cholesterol, 113 mg. Sodium, 9.3 g. Protein, 0.4 g. Fiber.

QUINOA SOUFFLE   **Serves 4**

Heartier than classical souffle, this one is great for brunch, lunch, supper or any other time you have a craving for something tasty.

- 1/2 cup Quinoa, thoroughly rinsed
- 1 cup Water
- 2 cups Low-Fat 2% Milk, hot

- 3 Egg Yolks
- 1/4 lb. shredded Swiss Cheese (1 cup packed)
- 2 tablespoons unsalted Butter or Margarine
- 1/4 teaspoon Salt
- 1/4 teaspoon White Pepper

- 3 Egg Whites

- 2 tablespoons grated Swiss Cheese
- 2 tablespoons grated Parmesan Cheese

Cook quinoa in water for 15 minutes. Add milk, cook uncovered until all milk has been absorbed. Remove from the heat and reserve.

Mix quinoa with egg yolks, cheese, butter or margarine, salt and pepper. Beat egg whites until stiff but not dry. Carefully fold into quinoa mixture. Transfer to a buttered 6-cup souffle dish, sprinkle cheeses on top and bake in a preheated 375° oven for 30 minutes or until puffed and golden brown. Serve immediately plain or with a tomato sauce on the side, as a main course to 4 or as a side dish to 8.

This souffle reheats very well in a 300° oven or in the microwave.

Per Serving: 324 Calories,   16.3 g. Fat,   243.9 mg. Cholesterol, 365 mg. Sodium,   21.7 g. Protein,   0.9 g. Fiber

QUINOA-PASTA WITH VEGETABLE SAUCE

Serves 4

This is a late summer dish when markets and gardens are bursting with fresh seasonal vegetables. Speedy preparation and short cooking time allows the freshly harvested vegetables to assert their flavorful best.

1/2 ounce Porccini Mushrooms

2 tablespoons Olive Oil
1 cup chopped fresh Mushrooms
1 cup diced (1/3-in.) Green Bell Pepper
1 cup diced (1/3-in.) Red Bell Pepper
2 cloves Garlic, minced
2 large ripe Tomatoes, peeled, seeded and chopped
2 tablespoons Tomato Paste
2 cups diced (1/3-in.) Zucchini
1 cup Corn Kernels, fresh or frozen (thawed)
1 Bay Leaf
1/2 teaspoon Sugar
1/2 teaspoon freshly ground Black Pepper
Coarse Salt

1/2 lb. Quinoa Fettuccine, cooked per package instructions
1/2 cup grated Parmesan Cheese

Soak porccini mushrooms in warm water for 30 minutes. Drain, rinse with cold water and chop.

In a large heavy skillet heat oil over medium high heat. Add fresh mushrooms and peppers, sauté for 5 minutes, stirring occasionally. Add porccini mushrooms, garlic, tomatoes and tomato paste, cook until tomatoes are saucy, about 10 minutes. Stir in zucchini, bay leaf, sugar and pepper. Reduce heat to low, cover and cook for 5 more minutes or until zucchini is tender. Season with salt if needed. Discard bay leaf, toss with pasta and parmesan cheese.

Serve immediately with extra Parmesan cheese on the side, if desired.

Sauce can be made ahead and reheated before cooking pasta.

Per Serving: 437 Calories, 17 g. Fat, 8.6 mg. Cholesterol, 295 mg. Sodium, 18.9 g. Protein, 2.8 g. Fiber

---

QUINOA-PASTA GRATINEED   **Serves 4**

Another excellent dish for people allergic to wheat flour. It can be used as a main course or as a side dish for grilled fish or chicken.

          2 tablespoons unsalted Butter or Margarine
          1 tablespoon minced Shallots or Scallions
          2 cups thinly sliced Mushrooms
          1 cup frozen Peas, thawed

          2 tablespoons Butter or Margarine
          1 tablespoon Cornstarch or Flour
          2 cups Low-Fat 2% Milk, hot
      1/4 teaspoon Coarse Salt
      1/4 teaspoon White Pepper
            Pinch of Nutmeg
            Pinch of Sugar

      1/2 lb. Quinoa Macaroni or Rotini, cooked as per package
            instructions
          1 cup grated Parmesan Cheese

In a skillet melt butter or margarine over medium high heat, add shallots or scallions and mushrooms, cook stirring until mushrooms are done, about 5 minutes. Add peas, cook for 1 minute. Set aside.

In a 2-quart saucepan melt butter or margarine over medium heat, stir in cornstarch until well blended, remove from the heat, whisk in hot milk, return to the heat and bring to the boil stirring constantly. Season with salt, pepper, nutmeg and sugar, lower the heat and simmer for a couple of minutes. Stir in mushroom mixture.

Butter a 6-cup shallow ovenproof dish and layer one half each of pasta, sauce and cheese. Repeat with the other half of each, finishing with a layer of cheese. Can be prepared ahead to this point, covered and refrigerated until needed. Bring to room temperature before baking. To serve, bake in the upper third of a preheated 375° oven for 20 minutes or until golden brown. Serve hot with a tossed salad as a main course to four, or as a side dish to eight people.

Per Serving: 515.5 Calories, 20.9 g. Fat, 25.0 mg. Cholesterol, 602.7 mg. Sodium, 21.2 g. Protein, 0.0 g. Fiber

QUINOA WITH CHICKEN, SPANISH STYLE

Serves 4

Tired of humdrum fried or baked chicken and mashed potatoes? This recipe combines the colorful earthiness of traditional Spanish cookery with the exotic flair and valuable nutrition of quinoa. A hearty main dish, its attractive presentation is sure to please lovers of the world's favorite poultry.

3/4	lb. skinless and boneless Chicken Breasts
1	Carrot, split lengthwise
4	cups Water
4	Chicken Bouillon Cubes
1	cup Quinoa, thoroughly rinsed
2	tablespoons Olive Oil
1	cup chopped Onion
1	small Green Bell Pepper, chopped
2	cloves Garlic, minced
1	large Tomato, peeled, seeded and chopped
1/2	teaspoon Paprika
1/4	teaspoon ground Cumin
1/2	teaspoon freshly ground Black Pepper
	Coarse Salt
1	cup cooked Beans (Pinto, Red, Garbanzo, etc.). Canned variety can be used if you don't mind higher sodium
1	2-oz. jar Pimento strips
12	small Black Olives

Put chicken, carrot, water and bouillon cubes in a 2-quart saucepan, bring to the boil over medium heat, skim, cover and simmer for 20 minutes or until chicken is done.

Remove chicken and carrot, strain broth, return 2 cups to saucepan, add quinoa, cover and cook for 15 minutes. Remove from the heat, fluff with a fork, cover and set aside.

While quinoa is cooking cut chicken in bite size pieces. Dice carrot. Set aside.

In a large skillet heat oil over medium heat, add onions and cook for 5 minutes, add green peppers, garlic and tomatoes, cook for 10 more minutes, covered. Stir in paprika, cumin, and pepper. Add chicken, carrots, and beans, simmer for 5 minutes to blend flavors. Season with salt and pepper to taste. Toss with quinoa, transfer to a heated serving platter, decorate with pimento strips and black olives. Serve immediately with a green salad and French bread.

Per Serving: 481 Calories, 15.7 g. Fat, 74.4 mg. Cholesterol, 634 mg. Sodium, 38.9 g. Protein, 64.6 g. Fiber.

QUINOA PILAFF   Makes 4 cups

- 2 tablespoons Vegetable Oil
- 1 whole clove Garlic
- 2 tablespoons minced Onion
- 1 cup Quinoa, thoroughly rinsed
- 2 cups Water, or Chicken Broth (will increase sodium!)

In a 2-quart saucepan heat oil, add garlic and onion and sauté over medium heat for a couple of minutes. Add quinoa, sauté, stirring for 5 minutes. Add water or chicken broth, bring to the boil, cover, reduce heat to low and simmer for 12 minutes or until all the water has been absorbed. If using water add salt to taste now. Remove from the heat, fluff, discard garlic clove, cover and let it stand 5 minutes before serving. Quinoa pilaff is a good substitute for rice pilaff.

To make quinoa pilaff with saffron, soften 1/4 teaspoon of crumbled saffron threads in 2 tablespoons warm water. Add to water or chicken broth and proceed as instructed.

Per Cup: 211 Calories, 48 g. Fat, 0.4 mg. Cholesterol, 12.5 mg. Sodium, 6 g. Protein, 1.7 g. Fiber.

SAVOY CABBAGE PATTIES   **Makes 8**

Lovers of Eastern European cooking will appreciate this easy recipe that gives all the taste and none of the hassle of traditional stuffed cabbage rolls. Forget arranging filling on fragile leaves and tying everything up with strings and try this simple patty mixture. Quinoa replaces the traditional white rice to help bind the patties as well as providing extra nutrition.

    4 cups finely chopped Savoy Cabbage

1/2 lb. lean Ground Meat (beef, chicken, turkey)
    2 Eggs, lightly beaten
1/4 teaspoon Garlic Powder
1/4 teaspoon Onion Powder
       pinch of Nutmeg
1/2 teaspoon Salt
1/4 teaspoon freshly ground Black Pepper
    2 tablespoons minced Fresh Parsley
    2 tablespoons Dry Bread Crumbs
    2 cups cooked Quinoa

    1 teaspoon Olive Oil

Steam or cook cabbage in boiling water for 10 minutes or until tender. Drain thoroughly and let it cool.

Mix ground meat with eggs, seasonings and bread crumbs, kneading until well blended. Add quinoa and cabbage, mix well and shape into 8 patties. In a large, heavy skillet heat oil over medium heat, add patties and cook until browned on both sides, about 4 minutes on each side. If frying pan is not large enough to hold 8 patties without crowding, sauté in two batches. Drain on paper towels and keep warm in a warming oven until ready to serve.

Per Patty: 144 Calories, 6.5 g. Fat, 920 mg. Cholesterol, 180 mg. Sodium, 18.8 g. Protein, 0.5 g. Fiber.

QUINOA, CHICKEN AND BLACK BEAN SALAD

Makes 8 cups

Even people who may be doubtful about quinoa are instantly won over with this brightly colorful salad. Appealing to the eye as well as the appetite, it is substantial enough to stand alone as a main course. It can be served both with or without meat.

3/4 cup Quinoa, thoroughly rinsed
3/4 lb. skinless and boneless Chicken Breast, cooked
  2 cups cooked Black Beans, canned variety can be used if you don't mind higher sodium.
  1 cup fresh or frozen Corn Kernels, cooked
1/2 cup chopped fresh Red Bell Pepper
1/2 cup chopped fresh Green Bell Pepper
1/2 cup chopped Red Onions
1/4 cup thinly sliced Scallions (use some of the green also)

Cilantro Vinaigrette
1/3 cup Olive Oil
  3 tablespoons Sherry Vinegar
  1 tablespoon Dijon Mustard
1/2 teaspoon Salt
1/2 teaspoon freshly ground Black Pepper
    pinch of Sugar
2-4 tablespoons fresh minced Cilantro Leaves (Coriander)

  6 Cherry Tomatoes (optional)

Cook quinoa in 6 cups of boiling salted water for 12 minutes or until grains are transparent throughout. Drain and transfer to a mixing bowl.

Cut chicken breast in small dice, should have about 2 cups. Add to quinoa and mix with beans, corn, peppers, onions and scallions.

In a jar fitted with a lid put vinegar, oil, mustard, salt, pepper and sugar. Shake for a few seconds until emulsified. Toss salad with vinaigrette, taste to see if more salt is needed, cover and refrigerate until needed. Just before serving toss with cilantro, transfer to a serving bowl, decorate with halved optional cherry tomatoes, or serve on a bed of greens.

Per 1 Cup: 276.2 Calories, 12.9 g. Fat, 27.5 mg. Cholesterol, 166 mg. Sodium, 17.2 g. Protein, 3.1 g. Fiber

21

WILD RICE WITH SHRIMP AND QUINOA SALAD

Makes 8 cups

This colorful main course salad is hearty with the nutritional punch of quinoa combined with wild rice. Shrimp add even more high-quality protein and flavor, while cilantro lends a south-of-the-border touch. Striking the keynote is a very light dressing that adds zest without masking the flavors of the individual ingredients. A fine party dish.

- 1/2 cup Wild Rice, thoroughly rinsed
- 1/2 cup Quinoa, thoroughly rinsed

- 12 Sun-Dried Tomatoes (or, a 2-oz. jar chopped Pimentos)
- 1 6-ounce pkg. frozen cooked small Shrimp, thawed, drained
- 1/2 cup chopped Red Onion
- 1 cup small seedless Green Grapes

- 1/3 cup Extra Virgin Olive Oil
- 2 tablespoons Sherry Vinegar
- 1/2 teaspoon Coarse Salt
- 1/2 teaspoon freshly ground Black Pepper
  pinch of Sugar
- 1/4 cup fresh minced Cilantro leaves (Coriander)
- 1 teaspoon fresh Lemon Juice (or more)

GARNISHES
- 1 medium Tomato cut into 8 wedges
- 1 medium Avocado peeled and cut into 8 wedges (opt.)

In a 2-quart saucepan put rice and 4 cups of water, bring to the boil, cover and cook over low heat for about 45 minutes or until rice is tender. Drain and set aside.

In another saucepan bring 4 cups of water to the boil, add quinoa, cook uncovered for 12 minutes or until grains are transparent throughout. Drain and set aside.

Blanch sun-dried tomatoes in boiling water for 1 minute. Drain and rinse thoroughly with cold water to remove sand. Chop coarsely.

In a large bowl combine rice, quinoa, sun-dried tomatoes, shrimp, onions and grapes.

In a jar fitted with a lid combine oil, vinegar, salt, pepper and sugar, shake until emulsified. Toss with quinoa mixture and coriander, add lemon juice to taste. Season with salt and pepper if needed. Cover and chill.

To serve transfer to a glass bowl, decorate with tomato and optional avocado wedges. Sprinkle lemon juice on avocado.

Per 1 Cup: 213.6 Calories,   11.2 g. Fat,   41.6 mg. Cholesterol, 170.6 mg. Sodium, 8.1 g. Protein, 1.0 g. Fiber

KOREAN STYLE SALAD   Serves 4

Quinoa again demonstrates its versatility in this oriental variation. Quinoa and sprouts flavored with soy sauce and garlic on lettuce leaves combine to make a tasty alternative for the egg roll crowd. Excellent as a light lunch, this salad also complements any oriental-style meal.

> 2 cups cooked Quinoa
>
> 1 cup Sprouted Mung Beans or any variety of sprouts
>
> 1/4 cup finely chopped Scallions (some green included)
> 2 tablespoon Light Soy Sauce
> 1 tablespoon Sesame Seed Oil
> 1 tablespoon Rice or White Vinegar
> 1/2 teaspoon Sugar
> 1 clove Garlic, minced
> 1/4 teaspoon freshly ground Black Pepper
>   dash of Cayenne Pepper
> 1/3 cup Pine Nuts, lightly toasted
>
> Lettuce leaves

Blanch sprouts in boiling water for 1 minute. Drain well.

Combine scallions, soy sauce, sesame seed oil, vinegar, sugar, garlic, black pepper and cayenne. Toss with quinoa, sprouts and pine nuts. Chill for at least 1 hour before serving mounded on lettuce leaves.

Per Serving: 177 Calories, 10.3 g. Fat, 0.2 mg. Cholesterol, 250 mg. Sodium, 4.5 g. Protein, 1.5 g. Fiber.

CREAMY QUINOA   **Serves 4**

This polenta-like Peruvian dish is usually served as a side dish for beef stew. It is an ideal main course for a meatless meal, especially when served topped with a tomato sauce made with onions, green peppers and tomatoes.

> 1 cup Quinoa, thoroughly rinsed
> 2 cups Water
>
> 2 cups Low Fat 2% Milk
> 2 tablespoon unsalted Butter or Margarine
> 1/2 cup shredded Cheese (munster, feta or parmesan)
> Coarse Salt
> White pepper

Put quinoa and water in a heavy 2-qt. saucepan, bring to the boil over medium heat, cover and cook over low heat for 12 minutes, or until all the water has been absorbed. Add milk and cook, stirring, until creamy. Stir in butter or margarine and cheese, cook until cheese is melted, season with salt and pepper to taste. Transfer to a serving dish and serve hot, plain or topped with the sauce below, and grilled fish or chicken.

Per Serving: 313 Calories, 142 g. Fat, 22.9 mg. Cholesterol, 16.2 mg. Sodium, 11.2 g. Protein, 2.5 g. Fiber

PEPPER, ONION AND TOMATO SAUCE

> 2 tablespoons Olive Oil
> 1 medium Onion, thinly sliced
> 1 medium Green Bell Pepper, thinly sliced
> 1 large Tomato, peeled, seeded and thinly sliced
> 1/4 teaspoon freshly ground Black Pepper
> Coarse Salt
> Sugar

In a large frying pan heat oil over medium heat, add onions and sauté stirring occasionally until transparent, about 5 minutes. Add green pepper and tomatoes, cook for 20 minutes, covered, until mixture is saucy. Season with pepper, salt and sugar to taste.

92 Calories, 7.1 g. Fat, 0.0 Cholesterol, 7.0 mg. Sodium, 1.2 g. Protein, 1.1 g. Fiber

DINNER ROLLS

Makes 24

Quinoa flour, butter and eggs add substance to these hearty, yet light, yeast-raised dinner rolls that will appeal to any palate.

> 1 pkg. Active Dry Yeast
> 2 tablespoons Sugar
> 1/2 cup Warm Water (120°-130°)
>
> 1 cup Warm Water
> 1/4 lb. Unsalted Butter or Margarine, softened
>
> 1 cup Quinoa Flour
> 3 cups Unbleached All-Purpose Flour
> 1 teaspoon Coarse Salt
>
> 1 Egg, lightly beaten with 1 tablespoon Water

Dissolve yeast and sugar in warm water and allow to rest for about 5 minutes or until bubbly.

Put 1 cup of warm water in a large bowl; cut butter in 8 pieces and melt in warm water. Combine with yeast mixture.

Mix quinoa flour, unbleached flour and salt; stir one cup at a time into the mixture in the bowl, beating with a wooden spoon to make a soft dough. Turn out on a lightly floured board and knead until smooth and elastic. Form the dough into a ball and put in a buttered bowl, turning so the dough surface is covered with butter. Cover and put in a warm draft-free place to raise until doubled in volume.

Punch the dough down with your fist, turn out on a lightly floured surface and let rest for a few minutes. Pull off equal pieces of dough the size of a golf ball and shape into balls. Place on a buttered cookie sheet, about 2-inches apart and let the rolls raise again until almost doubled in size. Brush them with egg wash and bake in a preheated 375° oven for 15 minutes or until cooked through. Take one out and break it in half to see if it is cooked inside.

Per Roll: 112 Calories, 4.6 g. Fat, 11.5 mg. Cholesterol, 80.9 mg. Sodium, 3.2 g. Protein, 3.1 g. Fiber

---

Desserts
And
Drinks

QUINOA PUDDING
WITH CURRANTS

Makes 4 cups

Citrus zest provides the underlying flavor that will have the uninitiated inquiring about secret ingredients. In all appearances similar to rice pudding, the quinoa adds a nutty undertone.

4	cups Low-Fat 2% Milk
1/4	cup Sugar
1	Cinnamon stick
1	strip Lemon or Orange Zest
1	cup Quinoa, thoroughly rinsed
2	cups Water
1/4	cup Currants or Raisins
2	tablespoons Butter or Margarine (optional)
1	teaspoon Vanilla Extract
	Ground Cinnamon

Put milk, salt, sugar, cinnamon stick and lemon or orange zest in a 3-quart saucepan, bring to the boil over medium heat and simmer for 15 minutes. Discard cinnamon stick and zest.

Put quinoa and water in a heavy casserole, bring to the boil over medium heat, cover, and simmer for 15 minutes. Add milk and currants, cook uncovered over medium low heat, stirring occasionally, until creamy. As it thickens it will need more stirring so it doesn't stick to the bottom. Remove from the heat, stir in butter and vanilla. Transfer to individual serving dishes or to a large glass bowl. Cool to room temperature and serve sprinkled with ground cinnamon.

Per 1/2 Cup Serving: 187 Calories, 5.5 g. Fat, 2.2 mg. Cholesterol, 9.0 mg. Sodium, 4.5 g. Protein, 1.2 g. Fiber.

PINEAPPLE-QUINOA DESSERT　　Serves 8

The crunchy texture of quinoa and the refreshing taste of pineapple make this a very appealing combination.

> 1　cup Quinoa, thoroughly rinsed
> 2　cups Water
>
> 1　cup Low-Fat 2% Milk
> 1/3　cup Sugar
> 2　cups diced (1/4-in.) fresh Pineapple
> 1/4　teaspoon ground Cinnamon
>
> 2　tablespoons Cornstarch, mixed with
> 2　tablespoons Water
>
> 1　6-ounce container Plain Yogurt
> 1/2　teaspoon Vanilla Extract
> 2　tablespoons chopped Walnuts
> 8　Strawberries

Put quinoa and water in a heavy 2-quart saucepan, bring to the boil over medium heat, reduce the heat and cook for 12 minutes or until all the liquid has been absorbed. Add milk and sugar, cook for 5 minutes after it comes to the boil, add pineapple and cinnamon, cook until thickened, about 5 minutes. Stir in the cornstarch mixture and cook, stirring, for a couple of minutes or until thickened. Transfer to a bowl and let it cool.

Fold yogurt and vanilla extract into pineapple mixture, chill. Serve in dessert glasses topped with nuts and a strawberry.

Per Serving: 190 Calories, 3.8 g. Fat, 2.4 mg. Cholesterol, 33.5 mg. Sodium, 5.4 g. Protein, 1.5 g. Fiber

QUINOA FRUIT BARS   **Makes 24**

Cinnamon combines with cloves and anise to give these moist cake-like bars a decided holiday tone. But they're versatile enough to suit any occasion, and their virtual trail mix of nuts and dried fruit will be appreciated by stamina seekers from hikers to woodchoppers. A certain winner, with anyone, watch them disappear from your serving platter.

      1   cup Quinoa
      2   cups Water

      1   cup Brown Sugar
      1   cup Rice Flour, Cornstarch or Flour
      1   teaspoon Baking Powder
   1/2   teaspoon Baking Soda
      1   teaspoon ground Cinnamon
   1/2   teaspoon ground Cloves
   1/4   teaspoon Nutmeg
      1   teaspoon Anise seeds
   1/2   cup Raisins
   1/2   cup coarsely chopped Dates or Dry Apricots
   1/2   cup chopped Walnuts

   1/4   lb. Unsalted Butter or Margarine, melted
   1/2   cup Orange Juice
      2   teaspoons Vanilla extract
      3   Eggs, lightly beaten

         Confectioners' Sugar for dusting (optional)

Cook quinoa according to the **Basic Boiled Quinoa** recipe. Remove from the heat and let it cool.

In a bowl mix dry ingredients thoroughly. Add quinoa, butter or margarine, orange juice, vanilla and eggs, mix well. Transfer to a buttered and floured 13 x 9 inch baking pan. Bake in a preheated 350° oven for 45 minutes, or until a tooth pick inserted in the center comes out clean. Cool, cut into 24 bars and serve dusted with confectioners' sugar if desired.

Per Bar: 145 Calories,   64 g. Fat,   34 mg. Cholesterol,   52 mg. Sodium, 2.5 g. Protein,   0.4 g. Fiber

---

BROWN SUGAR NUT BALLS   **Makes 60**

Quinoa's talent for producing a flour with character is brought to the fore in these crunchy palate pleasers. Nuts counterpoint an airy texture.

- 1/2 lb. Unsalted Butter or Margarine, softened
- 1/2 cup (packed) Light Brown Sugar
- 2 teaspoons Vanilla Extract

- 2 cups Quinoa Flour, mixed with
- 1/2 cup finely Ground Almonds

- 1/2 cup Confectioners' Sugar for dusting

In the large bowl of an electric mixer beat the butter or margarine until fluffy. Add brown sugar and vanilla extract, beat until well blended. Gradually add the flour and nut mixture (add in about 3 parts). Chill the dough if too soft to handle. Shape into 1-inch balls or crescents. Place on ungreased cookie sheets and bake in a preheated 350° oven for 12 minutes or until lightly browned. Cool on racks and dust with confectioners' sugar while warm.

Per Cookie: 56 Calories, 3.7 g. Fat, 2 mg. Cholesterol, 3 mg. Sodium, 0.8 g. Protein, 0.25 g. Fiber.

QUINOA AND
CORNSTARCH DAINTIES

Makes 4 dozen

*Who says health food—or healthy food—can't make a good tasting snack?
Quinoa flour lightened with cornstarch makes a wonderful light cookie
that would be at home on the shelves of the finest pastry shops. Not too
sweet, these delights are airy and aromatic with vanilla, perfect for
afternoon coffee.*

        1/2 lb. unsalted Margarine, softened
        1/2 cup Confectioners' Sugar
          2 teaspoons Vanilla Extract
        1/2 cup Cornstarch
          1 cup Quinoa Flour

        1/2 cup Confectioners' sugar for dusting

   In the large bowl of a mixer beat margarine until fluffy. Add
sugar and vanilla extract, beat until well blended. Stir in cornstarch
and quinoa flour, (add in about 3 parts). Chill the dough for an
hour or until stiff enough to handle. Shape into 1-inch balls. Place
on ungreased cookie sheets about 2 inches apart. Dip the thines of a
fork in flour and press the balls to flatten. Repeat going across.

   Bake in a preheated 275° oven for 30 minutes or until cooked
throughout. Cookies should not color. Cool on racks and dust with
confectioner's sugar while warm.

Per Cookie: 55 Calories, 3.8 g. Fat, 0.0 Cholesterol, 1.0 mg. Sodium,
0.4 g. Protein, 0.1 g. Fiber.

ATOLE WITH ALMONDS
AND QUINOA
Makes 4 cups

From relaxing between ski runs to armchair adventuring by the fireside, everyone knows how hot chocolate boosts body and spirit. This frothy quinoa-based alternative adapted from Montezuma's favorite drink, atole, is not only a potent energy booster, but allows those unfortunates who suffer chocolate allergies to enjoy without qualm. Sometimes made with fruits, nuts, or even chilis, one cup of this substantial drink can carry you through to lunch without a need of a mid-morning snack.

       3 cups Low-Fat 2% Milk
       1 cup cooked Quinoa
    1/2 cup ground Almonds
       4 tablespoons Sugar
       1 Cinnamon stick
          Few drops Vanilla Extract

          Ground Cinnamon

   In a small heavy saucepan put milk, quinoa, almonds, sugar and cinnamon stick. Bring to the boil over medium low heat, simmer partially covered, stirring occasionally, for 15 minutes. Remove cinnamon stick and blend in the blender until smooth. Taste for sugar, add more if needed. Serve hot, sprinkled with ground cinnamon.

Per Cup: 216 Calories, 4.5 g. Fat, 18.5 mg. Cholesterol, 95.8 mg. Sodium, 4.0 g. Protein, 0.8 g. Fiber.

FRUIT-QUINOA DRINK   Serves 4

Since the time of the Aztecs and Incas, Latin Americans insist on traditional fruit drinks with lunch. While frequently made plain, a uniquely Latin American touch involves adding a grain thickener. The thickeners are characteristic of the native Indians who were excellent intuitive nutritionists. Quinoa is the perfect thickener and is recommended, even today, especially for people and children who might have an otherwise poor diet. Make it with any kind of berries, pineapple, mango, etc., or a combination of your favorite fruits. Experiment with the amount of fruit and sugar to suit your taste. Honey was the favorite sweetener of the Aztecs.

1-1/2	cups Raspberries (or strawberries, pineapple, etc.)
1/2	cup Cooked Quinoa
1/4	cup Sugar
2	cups Water
1	Cinnamon Stick

Fresh lemon Juice

Mix raspberries, quinoa, water, sugar and cinnamon in a non-reactive saucepan. Bring to the boil over medium heat, simmer for 10 minutes. Remove cinnamon stick and pureé in blender until smooth. Pass through a sieve, if desired, and season with lemon juice to taste and chill.

Per Serving: 89.6 Calories, 0.75 g. Fat, 0.05 mg. Cholesterol, 1.9 mg. Sodium, 1.25 g. Protein, 24.2 g. Fiber

NOTES

NOTES